VATICAN
COUNCIL II

POPE BENEDICT XVI
SPIRITUAL THOUGHTS SERIES

Edited by Lucio Coco
Preface by Pope Benedict XVI

United States Conference of Catholic Bishops
Washington, DC

First printing, September 2012
ISBN 978-1-60137-367-0

CONTENTS

very Council is born from the Church and returns to the Church.

Benedict XVI

PREFACE

"Thus, as I prepare myself for the service that is proper to the Successor of Peter, I also wish to confirm my determination to continue to put the Second Vatican Council into practice, following in the footsteps of my Predecessors and in faithful continuity with the 2,000-year tradition of the Church." These are the first words of Pope Benedict XVI following his election as pontiff, pronounced at the end of the Eucharistic concelebration with the cardinal electors (April 20, 2005). And on that occasion he added: "This very year marks the 40th anniversary of the conclusion of the Council (December 8, 1965). As the years have passed, the Conciliar Documents have lost none of their timeliness; indeed, their teachings are proving particularly relevant to the new situation of the Church and the current globalized society" (*ibid.*).

The pontificate of Benedict XVI is marked almost providentially by these two anniversaries: the fortieth of the conclusion of Vatican Council II (December 8, 1965), which coincides with the year of his election to the See of Peter, and the fiftieth of the beginning of the Council, this latter occasion being one that the Holy Father wished to commemorate with a Year of Faith beginning on October 11, the date of the opening of the conciliar assembly in 1962. This is how he recalls this event in the apostolic letter *Porta Fidei*, in which he illustrates its scope and significance: "It seemed to me that timing the launch of the Year of Faith to coincide with the fiftieth anniversary of the opening of the Second Vatican Council would provide a good opportunity to help people understand that the texts bequeathed by the Council Fathers, in the words of Blessed John Paul II, 'have lost nothing of their value or brilliance' (*Novo Millennio Ineunte*, no. 57)" (*Porta Fidei*, no. 5).

Benedict XVI himself is absolutely convinced of the impact and significance of this ecclesial event, so much so that a few months after his election he could confidently affirm that the Council "can be and can become increasingly powerful for the ever necessary renewal of the Church" (Benedict XVI, Address, December 22, 2005). The task that Vatican II set for itself was that of expressing in a new way a certain truth, that of Christ and the Church, and of communicating it to the people of today. The whole Council was animated by the intention of proclaiming and bringing to the contemporary person Christ, the light of the world (cf. Paul VI, Address, September 29, 1963). In the heart of the Church, Benedict XVI comments, casting a retrospective look over that period, had emerged "the impelling desire, awakened by the Spirit, *for a new epiphany of Christ in the world*" (Benedict XVI, Homily, January 6, 2007). The world in question was one that the modern age had radically changed, and that no longer fit within the established and now narrow coordinates of Eurocentrism, nor even within those indicated by the term "Western." What was needed was the elaboration of a new vision, not only economic and political, but also cultural and spiritual, capable of interpreting the new dynamics that the modern world presented.

Vatican II had to describe a pilgrim Church confronting itself and its inner components, reflecting on its hierarchy, on the liturgy, on the centrality of Sacred Scripture, and extending this to the surrounding world in which it is immersed and toward which it has the responsibility of bringing the living ferment of Christ. In this perspective, Benedict XVI recognizes the great pastoral wisdom with which each of his predecessors "steered the boat of Peter on the course of authentic conciliar renewal, ceaselessly working for the faithful interpretation and implementation of Vatican Council II" (Benedict XVI, *Angelus*, December 8, 2005). And the same can certainly be said about his own activity. Throughout his entire pontificate, in fact, he has welcomed all the fundamental conciliar requirements, making himself an untiring supporter of a missionary Church that brings Christ to people and commits itself to making divine salvation accessible to the people of today.

The interpretation of the Council that Benedict XVI proposes is always that of continuity. In his address to the Roman Curia of December 22, 2005, and therefore from the very beginning of his Magisterium, the pope insists precisely on this necessity of renouncing any logic of discontinuity in approaching the themes of the Council and favoring the "hermeneutic of reform," of "innovation in continuity," the only approach that can allow the good seed of faith, already sown, to continue growing and developing. An extensive extract of this important address on the manner of interpreting the Council is presented as an introduction to the present collection. No less do all of the other texts that are presented in the book represent an evident testimony to the efforts of the Holy Father to point out a line of continuity between the conciliar Church and that of all time. As Benedict XVI affirmed in that same address to the curia, "The Church, both before and after the Council, was and is the same Church, one, holy, catholic and apostolic, journeying on through time; she continues 'her pilgrimage amid the persecutions of the world and the consolations of God' (St. Augustine, *De Civitate Dei*, XVIII, 51, 2: PL 41, 614), proclaiming the death of the Lord until he comes (cf. *Lumen Gentium*, no. 8)."

In this perspective, Pope Benedict continually refers to the conciliar documents in order to restore to the Church that universal and prophetic breadth that Vatican II had envisioned for it, reflecting precisely upon its nature and constitution, that of being the "mystical Body of Christ" (*Lumen Gentium*, no. 8). It is Christ, in fact, who makes the Council itself relevant—if he did not permeate it through and through, how could all of its proceedings and documents still speak to us today? It is Christ who must come to bring life to the letter, otherwise it would be nothing but a scrawl undecipherable for the needs and demands that life presents to us today. Once again recalling the years of Vatican II, the Holy Father gives voice to a thought worthy of representing the seal and synthesis of that crucial experience in the history of the Church: "[In these fifty years] almost everything has changed, but the Lord's fidelity has remained. He is the same yesterday, today and for ever: and this is our certainty that paves our way to the future. The moment of memory, the moment of gratitude is also the moment of hope: *In te Domine speravi, non confundar in aeternum* [In you, O Lord, have I hoped, let me not be confounded forever] (Ps 31:2)" (Benedict XVI, Address, July 1, 2011).

Lucio Coco

INTRODUCTION

If we interpret and implement [the Council] guided by a right hermeneutic, it can be and can become increasingly powerful for the ever necessary renewal of the Church.

BENEDICT XVI

The Hermeneutic of the Council[1]

hat has been the result of the Council? Was it well received? What, in the acceptance of the Council, was good and what was inadequate or mistaken? What still remains to be done? No one can deny that in vast areas of the Church the implementation of the Council has been somewhat difficult, even without wishing to apply to what occurred in these years the description that St. Basil, the great Doctor of the Church, made of the Church's situation after the Council of Nicea: he compares her situation to a naval battle in the darkness of the storm, saying among other things: "The raucous shouting of those who through disagreement rise up against one another, the incomprehensible chatter, the confused din of uninterrupted clamoring, has now filled almost the whole of the Church, falsifying through excess or failure the right doctrine of the faith" (*De Spiritu Sancto,* XXX, 77; *PG* 32, 213 A; SCh 17 ff., p. 524).

---

1   This introduction is an excerpt from the December 22, 2005, address by Pope Benedict XVI to the Roman Curia offering them his Christmas greetings.

We do not want to apply precisely this dramatic description to the situation of the post-conciliar period, yet something from all that occurred is nevertheless reflected in it. The question arises: Why has the implementation of the Council, in large parts of the Church, thus far been so difficult?

Well, it all depends on the correct interpretation of the Council or—as we would say today—on its proper hermeneutics, the correct key to its interpretation and application. The problems in its implementation arose from the fact that two contrary hermeneutics came face to face and quarreled with each other. One caused confusion, the other, silently but more and more visibly, bore and is bearing fruit.

On the one hand, there is an interpretation that I would call "a hermeneutic of discontinuity and rupture"; it has frequently availed itself of the sympathies of the mass media, and also one trend of modern theology. On the other, there is the "hermeneutic of reform," of renewal in the continuity of the one subject-Church which the Lord has given to us. She is a subject which increases in time and develops, yet always remaining the same, the one subject of the journeying People of God.

The hermeneutic of discontinuity risks ending in a split between the pre-conciliar Church and the post-conciliar Church. It asserts that the texts of the Council as such do not yet express the true spirit of the Council. It claims that they are the result of compromises in which, to reach unanimity, it was found necessary to keep and reconfirm many old things that are now pointless. However, the true spirit of the Council is not to be found in these compromises but instead in the impulses toward the new that are contained in the texts.

These innovations alone were supposed to represent the true spirit of the Council, and starting from and in conformity with them, it would be possible to move ahead. Precisely because the texts would only imperfectly reflect the true spirit of the Council and its newness, it would be necessary to go courageously beyond the texts and make room for the newness in which the Council's deepest intention would be expressed, even if it were still vague.

In a word: it would be necessary not to follow the texts of the Council but its spirit. In this way, obviously, a vast margin was left open for the question on how this spirit should subsequently be defined and room was consequently made for every whim.

The nature of a Council as such is therefore basically misunderstood. In this way, it is considered as a sort of constituent that eliminates an old constitution and creates a new one. However, the Constituent Assembly needs a mandator and then confirmation by the mandator, in other words, the people the constitution must serve. The Fathers had no such mandate and no one had ever given them one; nor could anyone have given them one because the essential constitution of the Church comes from the Lord and was given to us so that we might attain eternal life and, starting from this perspective, be able to illuminate life in time and time itself.

Through the Sacrament they have received, Bishops are stewards of the Lord's gift. They are "stewards of the mysteries of God" (1 Cor 4:1); as such, they must be found to be "faithful" and "wise" (cf. Lk 12:41-48). This requires them to administer the Lord's gift in the right way, so that it is not left concealed in some hiding place but bears fruit, and the Lord may end by saying to the administrator: "Since you were dependable in a small matter I will put you in charge of larger affairs" (cf. Mt 25:14-30; Lk 19:11-27).

These Gospel parables express the dynamic of fidelity required in the Lord's service; and through them it becomes clear that, as in a Council, the dynamic and fidelity must converge.

The hermeneutic of discontinuity is countered by the hermeneutic of reform, as it was presented first by Pope John XXIII in his Speech inaugurating the Council on October 11, 1962, and later by Pope Paul VI in his Discourse for the Council's conclusion on December 7, 1965.

Here I shall cite only John XXIII's well-known words, which unequivocally express this hermeneutic when he says that the Council wishes "to transmit the doctrine, pure and integral, without any attenuation or distortion." And he continues: "Our duty is not only to guard this precious treasure, as if we were concerned only with antiquity, but to dedicate ourselves with an earnest will and without fear to that work which our era demands of us." It is necessary that "adherence to all the teaching of the Church in its entirety and preciseness" be presented in "faithful and perfect conformity to the authentic doctrine, which, however, should be studied and expounded through the methods of research and through the literary forms of modern thought. The substance of the ancient doctrine of the deposit of faith is one thing, and the way in which it is presented is another," retaining the same meaning and message (*The Documents of Vatican II*, Walter M. Abbott, SJ, p. 715).

It is clear that this commitment to expressing a specific truth in a new way demands new thinking on this truth and a new and vital relationship with it; it is also clear that new words can only develop if they come from an informed understanding of the truth expressed, and on the other hand, that a reflection on faith also requires that this faith be lived. In this regard, the program that Pope John XXIII proposed was extremely demanding, indeed, just as the synthesis of fidelity and dynamic is demanding.

However, wherever this interpretation guided the implementation of the Council, new life developed and new fruit ripened. Forty years after the Council, we can show that the positive is far greater and livelier than it appeared to be in the turbulent years around 1968. Today, we see that although the good seed developed slowly, it is nonetheless growing; and our deep gratitude for the work done by the Council is likewise growing.

Benedictus XVI

VATICAN
COUNCIL II

I. THE COMPASS
OF THE COUNCIL

1. *Timeliness*

Thus, as I prepare myself for the service that is proper to the Successor of Peter, I also wish to confirm my determination to continue to put the Second Vatican Council into practice, following in the footsteps of my Predecessors and in faithful continuity with the 2,000-year tradition of the Church. . . . As the years have passed, the Conciliar Documents have lost none of their timeliness; indeed, their teachings are proving particularly relevant to the new situation of the Church and the current globalized society.

First Message of His Holiness Benedict XVI at the end of
the Eucharistic concelebration with the members of the
College of Cardinals in the Sistine Chapel
April 20, 2005

2. *Motivations of the Council*

The whole of the Second Vatican Council was truly stirred by the longing to proclaim Christ, the Light of the world, to contemporary humanity. In the heart of the Church, from the summit of her hierarchy, emerged the impelling desire, awakened by the Spirit, *for a new epiphany of Christ in the world*, a world that the modern epoch had profoundly transformed and that, for the first time in history, found itself facing the challenge of a global civilization in which the center could no longer be Europe or even what we call the West and the North of the world. The need to work out a new world political and economic order was emerging but, at the same time and above all, one that would be both spiritual and cultural, that is, a renewed humanism. This observation became more and more obvious: a new world economic and political order cannot work unless there is a spiritual renewal, unless we can once again draw close to God and find God in our midst. Before the Second Vatican Council, the enlightened minds of Christian thinkers had already intuited and faced this epochal challenge. Well, at the beginning of the third millennium, we find ourselves in the midst of this phase of human history that now focuses on the word "globalization."

Homily
January 6, 2007

3. *Finality*

Precisely so as "to place the modern world in contact with the life-giving and perennial energies of the Gospel" (John XXIII, Apostolic Constitution *Humanae Salutis*, no. 3), the Second Vatican Council was convened. There the Church, on the basis of a renewed awareness of the Catholic tradition, took seriously and discerned, transformed and overcame the fundamental critiques that gave rise to the modern world, the Reformation and the Enlightenment. In this way the Church herself accepted and refashioned the best of the requirements of modernity by transcending them on the one hand, and on the other by avoiding their errors and dead ends. The Council laid the foundation for an authentic Catholic renewal and for a new civilization—"the civilization of love"—as an evangelical service to man and society.

Meeting with the world of culture
May 12, 2010

4. *Continuity*

Vatican II embraces the entire doctrinal history of the Church. Anyone who wishes to be obedient to the Council has to accept the faith professed over the centuries, and cannot sever the roots from which the tree draws its life.

Letter to the bishops of the Catholic Church
March 10, 2009

5. *Inheritance* (1)

We are all truly indebted . . . for this extraordinary ecclesial event. The multiple doctrinal legacy that we find in its Dogmatic Constitutions, Declarations and Decrees still stimulates us to deepen our knowledge of the Word of God in order to apply it to the Church in the present day, keeping clearly in mind the many needs of the men and women of the contemporary world who are extremely in need of knowing and experiencing the light of Christian hope.

Message to participants in the International Conference
October 28, 2008

6. *Inheritance* (2)

We have to rediscover the Council's great legacy. It is not a spirit reconstructed from texts but consists of the great Council texts themselves, reinterpreted today with the experiences we have had which have borne fruit in so many movements and so many new religious communities.

Meeting with clergy of the Dioceses of
Belluno-Feltre and Treviso
July 24, 2007

7. *Just hermeneutic*

If we interpret and implement [the Council] guided by a right hermeneutic, it can be and can become increasingly powerful for the ever necessary renewal of the Church.

Address to the members of the Roman Curia and prelature
December 22, 2005

II. THE CONSTITUTIONS

a) *Sacrosanctum Concilium*[2]

8. *Continuity*

In the history of the liturgy there is growth and progress, but no rupture.

> *Letter on the occasion of the publication of the*
> *Apostolic Letter* Summorum Pontificum
> *July 7, 2007*

9. *The Tradition of faith*

It is necessary above all not to neglect the common Catholic spirituality which is expressed in the Liturgy and in the great Tradition of faith. This seems to me to be very important. This point is also important with regard to the Council. We need not . . . live the hermeneutic of discontinuity, but rather the hermeneutic of renewal, which is the spirituality of continuity, of going ahead in continuity. This seems to me to be very important also as regards the Liturgy. . . .

---

2 *Constitution on the Sacred Liturgy* (December 4, 1963)

We must accept newness but also love continuity, and we must see the Council in this perspective of continuity. This will also help us in mediating between the generations in their way of communicating the faith.

> *Meeting with the clergy of the Diocese of Rome*
> *March 2, 2006*

10. *The figure of Christ*

"The real nature of the true Church . . . is essentially both human and divine, visible but endowed with invisible realities, zealous in action and dedicated to contemplation, present in the world, but as a pilgrim, so constituted that in her the human is directed toward and subordinated to the divine, the visible to the invisible, action to contemplation, and this present world to that city yet to come, the object of our quest" (*Sacrosanctum Concilium*, no. 2). If, in the Liturgy the figure of Christ who is its principle and is really present to make it effective were not to emerge we should no longer have the Christian liturgy, completely dependent upon the Lord and sustained by his creative presence.

> *Address to the bishops of the*
> *Episcopal Conference of Brazil*
> *April 15, 2010*

11. *Liturgy and prayer*

In the first place, it is important . . . to take care of the liturgy, which, as the Second Vatican Council teaches: "daily builds up those who are in the Church . . . into a holy temple of the Lord . . . to the mature measure of the fullness of Christ. At the same time it marvelously increases their power to preach Christ" (Constitution on the Sacred Liturgy *Sacrosanctum Concilium*, no. 2). May an intense life of prayer and assiduous participation in the liturgy continue to be your priority commitment, as individuals and as a sodality.

> *Address to the members of the Ss. Peter*
> *and Paul Association*
> *June 17, 2006*

12. *Care*

The Constitution *Sacrosanctum Concilium* stresses that it is in the Liturgy that the mystery of the Church is made manifest in its grandeur and its simplicity (cf. Introduction, no. 2). Thus it is important that priests take care in liturgical celebrations, particularly the Eucharist, to ensure that they permit a profound communion with the Living God, Father, Son and Holy Spirit. It is necessary that celebrations take place with respect for the Church's liturgical tradition, with the active participation of the faithful, according to each one's specific role, uniting personally with Christ's Paschal Mystery.

> *Address to the bishops of the*
> *Episcopal Conference of Belgium*
> *May 8, 2010*

13. *Liturgy, living reality*

There is no opposition between the liturgy renewed by the Second Vatican Council and this liturgy. On each day [of the Council], the Council Fathers celebrated Mass in accordance with the ancient rite and, at the same time, they conceived of a natural development for the liturgy within the whole of this century, for the liturgy is a living reality that develops but, in its development, retains its identity. Thus, there are certainly different accents, but nevertheless [there remains] a fundamental identity that excludes a contradiction, an opposition between the renewed liturgy and the previous liturgy. In any case, I believe that there is an opportunity for the enrichment of both parties. On the one hand the friends of the old liturgy can and must know the new saints, the new prefaces of the liturgy, etc. . . . On the other, the new liturgy places greater emphasis on common participation, but it is not merely an assembly of a certain community, but rather always an act of the universal Church in communion with all believers of all times, and an act of worship. In this sense, it seems to me that there is a mutual enrichment, and it is clear that the renewed liturgy is the ordinary liturgy of our time.

Interview of the Holy Father
September 12, 2008

14. *The worship of images*

The new step is that this mysterious God liberates us from the inflation of images and from an age filled with images of divinities and gives us the freedom of vision of the essential.

God appears with a face, a body, a human history, which is at the same time divine. It is a history that continues in the history of saints, martyrs, saints of charity, of the word, who are always an explanation, a continuation of his divine and human life in the Body of Christ and give us the fundamental images in which—over and above superficial images that conceal reality—we can open our gaze to Truth itself. In this regard I find the iconoclastic period of the post-conciliar years excessive; yet it had a meaning of its own since it may have been necessary to be freed from the superficiality of too many images.

Meeting with the clergy of the Diocese of Rome
February 7, 2008

15. *Liturgical reform*

The beneficial influence on the Church's life of the liturgical renewal . . . began with the Second Vatican Ecumenical Council. . . . There were many expressions of appreciation. The difficulties and even the occasional abuses which were noted, it was affirmed, cannot overshadow the benefits and the validity of the liturgical renewal, whose riches are yet to be fully explored. Concretely, the changes which the Council called for need to be understood within the overall unity of the historical development of the rite itself, without the introduction of artificial discontinuities.

Apostolic exhortation Sacramentum Caritatis, *no. 3*

16. *Beyond the conciliar reform*

The Liturgy of the Church goes beyond the "conciliar reform" itself (cf. *Sacrosanctum Concilium*, no. 1), whose aim, in fact, was not primarily to change the rites and the texts, but rather to renew mentalities and to put at the center of Christian life and ministry the celebration of the Paschal Mystery of Christ. Unfortunately, perhaps, we too, Pastors and experts, understood the Liturgy as an *object* to be reformed rather than a *subject* capable of renewing Christian life, since "a very close and organic bond exists between the renewal of the Liturgy and the renewal of the whole life of the Church. The Church not only acts but also expresses herself in the Liturgy and draws from the Liturgy the strength for her life." Blessed John Paul II reminds us of this in *Vicesimus Quintus Annus*, in which the Liturgy is seen *as the vibrant heart of all ecclesial activity*.

> *Address on the 50th anniversary of the Pontifical*
> *Athenaeum of Saint Anselm*
> *May 6, 2011*

b) *Lumen Gentium*[3]

17. *Intimate union*

It is necessary to perceive the Church, as she is presented to us by the Second Vatican Council, as a sacrament of intimate union with God, hence, of unity among all of us and, lastly, among the whole human race (cf. *Lumen Gentium*, no. 1).

General audience
December 12, 2007

18. *Mystery of communion*

In a society fraught between globalization and individualism, the Church is called to offer a witness of *koinonìa*, of communion. This reality does not come "from below" but is a mystery which, so to speak, "has its roots in Heaven," in the Triune God himself. It is he, in himself, who is the eternal dialogue of love which was communicated to us in Jesus Christ and woven into the fabric of humanity and history to lead it to fullness. And here then is the great synthesis of the Second Vatican Council: the Church, mystery of communion, "in Christ is in the nature of sacrament—a sign and instrument, that is, of communion with God and of unity among all men" (Dogmatic Constitution on the Church, *Lumen Gentium*, no. 1).

Homily on the Solemnity of the Most Holy Trinity
May 18, 2008

---

3   *Dogmatic Constitution on the Church* (November 21, 1964).

19. *The Church, mystical Body of Christ*

It seems to me that we must interiorize this ecclesiology far more, that of *Lumen Gentium* and of *Ad Gentes*, which is also an ecclesiological Document, as well as the ecclesiology of the minor Documents and of *Dei Verbum*. By interiorizing this vision we can also attract our people to this vision, which understands that the Church is not merely a large structure, one of these supranational bodies that exist. Although she is a body, the Church is the Body of Christ, hence, she is a spiritual body, as St. Paul said. She is a spiritual reality. I think this is very important: that people see that the Church is not a supranational organization nor an administrative body or power, that she is not a social agency, but indeed that although she does social and supranational work, she is a spiritual body.

Meeting with the clergy of the Diocese of Rome
February 22, 2007

20. *The People of God*

The two concepts "People of God" and "Body of Christ" complete each other and together form the New Testament concept of Church. And whereas "People of God" expresses the continuity of the Church's history, "Body of Christ" expresses the universality inaugurated in the Cross and in the Lord's Resurrection. For us Christians, therefore, "Body of Christ" is not only an image, but a true concept, because Christ makes us the gift of his real Body, not only an image of it. Risen, Christ unites us all in the Sacrament to make us one Body. Thus the concept "People of God" and "Body of

Christ" complete one another: in Christ we really become the People of God. "People of God" therefore means "all," from the Pope to the most recently baptized child. Subsequent to the Council this ecclesiological doctrine met with acceptance on a vast scale and thanks be to God an abundance of good fruit developed in the Christian community. However we must also remember that the integration of this doctrine in procedures and its consequent assimilation in the fabric of ecclesial awareness did not happen always and everywhere without difficulty and in accordance with a correct interpretation. As I was able to explain in my Discourse to the Roman Curia on December 22, 2005, an interpretative current, claiming to refer to a presumed "spirit of the Council," sought to establish a discontinuity and even to distinguish between the Church before and the Church after the Council, at times even crossing the very boundaries that exist objectively between the hierarchical ministry and the responsibilities of the lay faithful in the Church. The notion of "People of God" in particular was interpreted by some, in accordance with a purely sociological vision, with an almost exclusively horizontal bias that excluded the vertical reference to God. This position was in direct contrast with the word and spirit of the Council which did not desire a rupture, another Church, but rather a true and deep renewal in the continuity of the one subject Church which grows in time and develops but always remains identical, the one subject of the People of God on pilgrimage.

Speech at the inauguration of the
Ecclesial Convention of the Diocese of Rome
May 26, 2009

21. *The laity*

The Council has offered wise directives so that "the faithful should learn to distinguish carefully between the rights and the duties which they have as belonging to the Church and those which fall to them as members of the human society," and "they will strive to unite the two harmoniously, remembering that in every temporal affair they are to be guided by a Christian conscience, since not even in temporal business may any human activity be withdrawn from God's dominion" (*Lumen Gentium*, no. 36). For this very reason the Council exhorts lay believers to welcome "what is decided by the Pastors as teachers and rulers of the Church," and then recommends that "Pastors . . . should recognize and promote the dignity and responsibility of the laity in the Church. They should willingly use their prudent advice" and concludes that "[m]any benefits for the Church are to be expected from this familiar relationship between the laity and the Pastors" (cf. *Lumen Gentium*, no. 37).

> *Address to the members of the Pontifical*
> *Academy for Life*
> *February 24, 2007*

22. *New charisms*

In various Documents the Second Vatican Council makes reference to the Movements and new Ecclesial Communities, especially in the Dogmatic Constitution *Lumen Gentium*, where we read: "Whether these charisms be very remarkable or more simple and widely diffused, they are to be received with thanksgiving and consolation" (no. 12).

Later the *Catechism of the Catholic Church* also emphasized the value and importance of new charisms in the
Church, whose authenticity however is guaranteed by their
openness to subject themselves to the discernment of the
ecclesiastic authority (cf. no. 2003). Precisely because we
are assisting at a promising flowering of Movements and
Ecclesial Communities, it is important that Pastors exercise
prudent and wise discernment in their regard. I sincerely
hope that dialogue between Pastors and Ecclesial Movements intensifies at all levels: parish, diocesan and with
the Apostolic See. I know that opportune ways are being
studied to give Pontifical recognition to the New Movements and Ecclesial Communities and many have already
received it. This fact—the recognition or establishment of
international associations on the part of the Holy See for
the universal Church—Pastors, especially Bishops, cannot
fail to take into account in their dutiful discernment that
lies within their competence (cf. Congregation for Bishops,
Directory for the Pastoral Ministry of Bishops *Apostolo-
rum Successores*, ch. 4, 8).

> *Address to participants in the 13th international
> conference of the Catholic Fraternity of Charismatic
> Covenant Communities and Fellowship
> October 31, 2008*

23. *The faithful's vocation to holiness*

The Second Vatican Council highlights the universal call
to holiness when it affirms: "The followers of Christ are
called by God, not because of their works, but according to

his own purpose and grace. They are justified in the Lord Jesus, because in the Baptism of faith they truly become sons of God and sharers in the divine nature. In this way, they are really made holy" (*Lumen Gentium*, no. 40). Within the framework of this universal call, Christ, the High Priest, in his solicitude for the Church calls persons in every generation who are to care for his people. In particular, he calls to the ministerial priesthood men who are to exercise a fatherly role, the source of which is within the very fatherhood of God (cfr. Eph 3:14). The mission of the priest in the Church is irreplaceable.

Message for the 43rd World Day of Prayer for Vocations
May 7, 2006

24. Sacrament of salvation

As the Second Vatican Council expresses it, the Church is the "universal sacrament of salvation" (*Lumen Gentium*, no. 48), existing for sinners, for us, in order to open up to us the path of conversion, healing and life. That is the Church's great perennial mission, entrusted to her by Christ.

Homily at Mass at the Olympic Stadium in Berlin
September 22, 2011

25. Mary in the mystery of the Church

Between Mary and the Church there is indeed a connatural relationship that was strongly emphasized by the Second Vatican Council in its felicitous decision to place the treatment of the Blessed Virgin at the conclusion of the Constitution on the Church, *Lumen Gentium*.

Homily on the Solemnity of the Annunciation of the Lord
March 25, 2006

c) *Dei Verbum*[4]

26. *Listening*

The Dogmatic Constitution *Dei Verbum*, whose drafting I personally witnessed as a young theologian, taking part in the lively discussions that went with it, begins with a deeply meaningful sentence: "*Dei Verbum religiose audiens et fidenter proclamans, Sacrosancta Synodus . . .*" ["Hearing the Word of God with reverence, and proclaiming it with faith, the Sacred Synod . . ."] (no. 1). With these words the Council points out a descriptive aspect of the Church: she is a community that listens to and proclaims the Word of God. The Church does not live on herself but on the Gospel, and in the Gospel always and ever anew finds the directions for her journey. This is a point that every Christian must understand and apply to himself or herself: only those who first listen to the Word can become preachers of it. Indeed, they must not teach their own wisdom but the wisdom of God, which often appears to be foolishness in the eyes of the world (cf. 1 Cor 1:23).

> *Address at the commemoration of the*
> *40th anniversary of* Dei Verbum
> *September 16, 2005*

---

4 *Dogmatic Constitution on Divine Revelation* (November 18, 1965).

27. *Pillar*

Dei Verbum . . . is one of the pillars on which the entire Council is built. It addresses Revelation and its transmission, the inspiration and interpretation of Sacred Scripture and its fundamental importance in the life of the Church. Gathering the fruits of the theological renewal that preceded it, Vatican II put Christ at the center, presenting him as "both the mediator and the sum total of Revelation" (no. 2). Indeed, the Lord Jesus, the Word made flesh who died and rose, brought to completion the work of salvation, consisting of deeds and words, and fully manifested the face and will of God so that no new public revelation is to be expected until his glorious return (cf. no. 3). The Apostles and their successors, the Bishops, are depositories of the message that Christ entrusted to his Church so that it might be passed on in its integrity to all generations. Sacred Scripture of the Old and New Testaments and sacred Tradition contain this message, whose understanding develops in the Church with the help of the Holy Spirit. This same Tradition makes known the integral canon of the sacred Books. It makes them directly understandable and operative so that God, who has spoken to the Patriarchs and Prophets, does not cease to speak to the Church and through her, to the world (cf. no. 8).

Angelus
November 6, 2005

28. *The Apostolic Tradition*

This topic of Tradition is so important that I would like to reflect upon it again today: indeed, it is of great importance for the life of the Church. The Second Vatican Council pointed out in this regard that Tradition is primarily *apostolic* in its origins: "God graciously arranged that the things he had once revealed for the salvation of all peoples should remain in their entirety, throughout the ages, and be transmitted to all generations. Therefore, Christ the Lord, in whom the entire Revelation of the Most High God is summed up (cf. 2 Cor 1:20; and 3:16–4, 6), commanded the Apostles to preach the Gospel . . . and communicate the gifts of God to all men. This Gospel was to be the source of all saving truth and moral discipline" (Dogmatic Constitution on Divine Revelation *Dei Verbum*, no. 7). The Council noted further that this was faithfully done "by the Apostles who handed on, by the spoken word of their preaching, by the example they gave, by the institutions they established, what they themselves had received—whether from the lips of Christ, from his way of life and his works, or whether they had learned it at the prompting of the Holy Spirit" (*ibid.*). The Council adds that there were "other men associated with the Apostles, who, under the inspiration of the same Holy Spirit, committed the message of salvation to writing" (*ibid.*).

General audience
May 3, 2006

29. *Twofold banquet*

"The Church," as the Second Vatican Council highlights, "has always venerated the divine Scriptures as she venerated the Body of the Lord, insofar as she never ceases, particularly in the sacred liturgy to partake of the bread of life and to offer it to the faithful from the one table of the Word of God and the Body of Christ" (*Dei Verbum*, no. 21). The Council rightly concludes: "Just as from constant attendance at the Eucharistic mystery the life of the Church draws increase, so a new impulse of spiritual life may be expected from increased veneration of the Word of God, which 'stands for ever'" (*Dei Verbum*, no. 26). May the Lord grant that we approach with faith the twofold banquet of the Body and Blood of Christ. May Mary Most Holy, who "kept all these things, pondering them in her heart" (Lk 2:19) obtain this for us. May she teach us to listen to the Scriptures and meditate upon them in an inner process of maturation that never separates the mind from the heart.

Homily at Mass for the opening of the 12th Ordinary
General Assembly of the Synod of Bishops
October 5, 2008

30. *Biblical exegesis* (1)

The Conciliar Constitution *Dei Verbum* still illumines the work of Catholic exegetes today and invites Pastors and faithful to be more regularly nourished at the table of the word of God. In this regard the Council recalls first of all that God is the Author of Sacred Scripture: "The divinely revealed realities, which are contained and presented in the text of Sacred Scripture, have been written down under the inspiration of the Holy Spirit. For Holy Mother Church relying on the faith of the apostolic age, accepts as sacred and canonical the Books of the Old and the New Testaments, whole and entire, with all their parts, on the grounds that, written under the inspiration of the Holy Spirit they have God as their author, and have been handed on as such to the Church herself" (*Dei Verbum*, no. 11). Therefore since all that the inspired authors or hagiographers state is to be considered as said by the Holy Spirit, the invisible and transcendent Author, it must consequently be acknowledged that "the books of Scripture, firmly, faithfully and without error, teach that truth which God, for the sake of our salvation, wished to see confided to the sacred Scriptures" (*ibid.*, no. 11).

Address to members of the Pontifical Biblical Commission
April 23, 2009

31. *Biblical exegesis* (2)

One aspect very deeply reflected upon was the relationship between the Word and words, that is, between the Divine Word and the Scriptures that express it. As the Second Vatican Council teaches in the Constitution *Dei Verbum* (no. 12), a good biblical exegesis demands both the historical-critical and theological methods since Sacred Scripture is the Word of God in human words. This means that every text must be read and interpreted keeping in mind the unity of the whole of Scripture, the living tradition of the Church and the light of the faith. If it is true that the Bible is also a literary work—even the great codex of universal culture—it is also true that it should not be stripped of the divine element but must be read in the same Spirit in which it was composed. Scientific exegesis and *lectio divina* are therefore both necessary and complementary in order to seek, through the literal meaning, the spiritual meaning that God wants to communicate to us today.

Angelus
October 26, 2008

32. *Biblical exegesis* (3)

From the correct presentation of the divine inspiration and truth of Sacred Scripture certain norms derive that directly concern its interpretation. The Constitution *Dei Verbum* itself, after stating that God is the author of the Bible, reminds us that in Sacred Scripture God speaks to man in a human fashion and this divine-human synergy is very important: God really speaks to men and women in a human way. For a correct interpretation of Sacred Scripture it is therefore necessary to seek attentively what the hagiographers have truly wished to state and what it has pleased God to express in human words. "The words of God, expressed in the words of men, are in every way like human language, just as the Word of the eternal Father, when he took on himself the flesh of human weakness, became like men" (*Dei Verbum*, no. 13). Moreover, these indications, very necessary for a correct historical and literary interpretation as the primary dimension of all exegesis, require a connection with the premises of the teaching on the inspiration and truth of Sacred Scripture. In fact, since Scripture is inspired, there is a supreme principal for its correct interpretation without which the sacred writings would remain a dead letter of the past alone: Sacred Scripture "must be read and interpreted with its divine authorship in mind" (*ibid.*, no. 12). . . . The scientific study of the sacred texts is important but is not sufficient in itself because it would respect only the human dimension. To respect the coherence of the Church's faith, the Catholic exegete must be attentive to perceiving the Word of God in these texts, within the faith of the Church herself. If this indispensable reference point is missing, the exegetical research would be incomplete, losing sight of its principal goal, and risk being reduced to a purely literary interpretation in which the true Author—God—no longer appears.

Address to members of the Pontifical Biblical Commission
April 23, 2009

33. Theological exegesis

Dei Verbum, no. 12, offers two methodological guidelines for suitable exegetical work. Firstly, it confirms the necessity of using the historical-critical method, of which it briefly describes the essential elements. This necessity is the result of the Christian principle formulated in Jn 1:14, "*Verbum caro factum est.*" Historical fact is a constituent dimension of the Christian faith. The history of salvation is not mythology but rather true history, and is therefore to be studied alongside serious historical research methods. Nevertheless, this history has another dimension, that of divine action. *Dei Verbum*, consequentially, speaks of a second methodological level necessary for the correct interpretation of the words that are simultaneously human words and the divine Word. . . . Only where the two methodological levels, both historical-critical and theological, are observed can one speak of theological exegesis, of an exegesis adequate to this Book. While at the first level, academic exegetical work is currently being done to an extremely high standard and provides us real help, the same cannot be said of the other level. Often this second level . . . appears almost absent. And this has rather grave consequences. The first consequence of the absence of this second methodological level is that the Bible becomes solely a history book. Moral consequences can be drawn from it, history can be learned from it, but the Book as such speaks of history alone and exegesis is no longer truly theological but instead becomes purely historiographical, literary history. This is the first consequence: the Bible remains in the past, speaks only of the past. The second consequence is even graver: where the hermeneutics of faith explained in *Dei Verbum* disappear, another type of hermeneutics will appear by necessity—a hermeneutics that is secularist, positivist, the key fundamental of which is the conviction that the Divine does not appear in human history.

Address during the 14th general
congregation of the Synod of Bishops
October 14, 2008

34. *Impact*

We are grateful to God that in recent times, and thanks to the impact made by the Dogmatic Constitution *Dei Verbum*, the fundamental importance of the Word of God has been deeply re-evaluated. From this has derived a renewal of the Church's life, especially in her preaching, catechesis, theology and spirituality, and even in the ecumenical process. The Church must be constantly renewed and rejuvenated and the Word of God, which never ages and is never depleted, is a privileged means to achieve this goal.

Address at the commemoration of the
40th anniversary of Dei Verbum
September 16, 2005

d) *Gaudium et Spes*[5]

35. *The signs of the times*

The Second Vatican Council, in the Pastoral Constitution *Gaudium et Spes*, also invites believers to examine the signs of the times in the light of the Gospel, in order to find in them a manifestation of God's action (cf. nos. 4, 11). This attitude of faith leads men and women to recognize the power of God who works in history and thus to open themselves to feeling awe for the name of the Lord. In biblical language, in fact, this "fear" is not fright, it does not denote fear, for fear of God is something quite different. It is recognition of the mystery of divine transcendence. Thus, it is at the root of faith and is interwoven with love. Sacred Scripture says in Deuteronomy: "What does the Lord, your God, ask of you but to fear the Lord, your God, and . . . to love . . . the Lord, your God, with all your heart and all your soul" (cf. Dt 10:12).

General audience
May 11, 2005

36. *The contemporary world*

The contemporary world continues to present contradictions so clearly outlined by the Fathers of the Second Vatican Council (cf. *Gaudium et Spes*, nos. 4-10): we see a humanity that would like to be self-sufficient, where more

---

5   *On the Church in the Modern World* (December 7, 1965).

than a few consider it almost possible to do without God in order to live well; and yet how many seem sadly condemned to face the dramatic situations of an empty existence, how much violence there still is on the earth, how much solitude weighs on the soul of the humanity of the communications era! In a word, it seems that today there is even loss of the "sense of sin," but in compensation the "guilt complex" has increased. Who can free the heart of humankind from this yoke of death if not the One who by dying overcame for ever the power of evil with the omnipotence of divine love? As St. Paul reminded the Christians of Ephesus: "God, who is rich in mercy, out of the great love with which he loved us, even when we were dead through our trespasses, made us alive together with Christ" (Eph 2:4).

Address to participants in the Course on the Internal
Forum organized by the Tribunal of the Apostolic
Penitentiary
March 16, 2007

37. *Religious sense*

Modern culture has legitimately emphasized the autonomy of the human person and earthly realities, thereby developing a perspective dear to Christianity, the Incarnation of God. However, as the Second Vatican Council clearly asserted, if this autonomy leads us to think that "material being does not depend on God and that man can use it as if it had no relation to its Creator," a deep imbalance will result, for "without a Creator there can be no creature"

(*Gaudium et Spes*, no. 36). It is significant that in the passage cited, the conciliar Document states that this capacity to recognize the voice and manifestation of God in the beauty of creation belongs to all believers, regardless of their religion. From this we can conclude that full respect for life is linked to a *religious sense*, to the inner attitude with which the human being faces reality, as master or as custodian. Moreover, the word "*respect*" derives from the Latin word *respicere*, to look at, and means a way of looking at things and people that leads to recognizing their substantial character, not to appropriate them but rather to treat them with respect and to take care of them. In the final analysis, if creatures are deprived of their reference to God as a transcendent basis, they risk being at the mercy of the will of man who, as we see, can make an improper use of it.

Homily at the parish of St. Anne at the Vatican
February 5, 2006

38. History and creatureliness

I remember when the conciliar Constitution *Gaudium et Spes* was discussed. On the one hand, there was a recognition of the new, of newness, the "yes" of the Church to the new epoch with its innovations, its "no" to the romanticism of the past, a proper and necessary "no." However, the Fathers—proof of this is also in the text—also said that in spite of this, in spite of the necessary willingness to move forward and even leave behind other things that were dear to us, there is something that does not change, because it is the human being himself, his being as a creature. Man is not completely historical. The absolutizing of historicism, in the sense that man is only and always a creature, the product of a certain period, is not true. His nature as a creature exists, and it is precisely this that gives us the possibility to live through change and to retain our identity.

Meeting with the clergy of the Diocese of Rome
March 2, 2006

39. Encounter

Our answer is the proclamation of God, the friend of man, who through Jesus became close to each one of us. The transmission of the faith is an inalienable part of the integral formation of the person, because in Jesus Christ the hope of a fulfilled life is realized: as the Second Vatican Council teaches, "whoever follows Christ, the perfect man, becomes himself more a man" (*Gaudium et Spes*, no. 41). The personal encounter with Jesus is the key to understanding the importance of God in our daily existence, the secret of how to live it in brotherly love, the condition that makes it possible to pick ourselves up after a fall and to move towards constant conversion.

Address to the General Assembly of the
Italian Episcopal Conference
May 27, 2010

40. *Consistency*

I would like to recall the words of the Pastoral Constitution *Gaudium et Spes*: consistency between faith and conduct, between Gospel and culture. The Council exhorts the faithful "to perform their duties faithfully in the spirit of the Gospel. It is a mistake to think that, because we have here no lasting city, but seek the city which is to come, we are entitled to shirk our earthly responsibilities; this is to forget that by our faith we are bound all the more to fulfill these responsibilities according to the vocation of each one" (no. 43). . . . Let us make our own the Council's desire that the faithful may be increasingly anxious to "carry out their earthly activity in such a way as to integrate human, domestic, professional, scientific and technical enterprises with religious values, under whose supreme direction all things are ordered to the glory of God" (*ibid.*) and thus for humanity's good.

General audience
October 31, 2007

41. *Culture*

The Second Vatican Ecumenical Council paid great attention to culture, and the Pastoral Constitution on the Church in the Modern World *Gaudium et Spes* dedicated a special chapter to it (cf. nos. 53-62). The Council Fathers were concerned to point out the perspective in which the Church views and addresses the promotion of culture, considering this task as one of the "more urgent problems deeply affecting the human race" (*ibid.*, no. 46). In her relations with the world of culture, the Church always places man at the center, both as the author of cultural activity and the one to whom it is destined.

*Address to the officials of the
Pontifical Council for Culture
June 15, 2007*

42. *Marriage* (1)

And Jesus added: "So they are no longer two but one. What therefore God has joined together, let not man put asunder" (Mk 10:8-9). This is God's original plan, as the Second Vatican Council also recalled in the Constitution *Gaudium et Spes*: "The intimate partnership of life and love which constitutes the married state has been established by the Creator and endowed by him with its own proper laws: it is rooted in the contract of its partners . . . God himself is the author of marriage" (no. 48).

Angelus
October 8, 2006

43. *Marriage* (2)

It seems to some that the conciliar teaching on marriage, and in particular, the description of this institution as "*intima communitas vitae et amoris*" [*the intimate partnership of life and love*] (Pastoral Constitution on the Church in the Modern World, *Gaudium et Spes*, no. 48), must lead to a denial of the existence of an indissoluble conjugal bond because this would be a question of an "ideal" to which "normal Christians" cannot be "constrained." In fact, the conviction that the pastoral good of the person in an irregular marital situation requires a sort of canonical regularization, independently of the validity or nullity of his/her marriage, independently, that is, of the "truth" of his/her personal status, has also spread in certain ecclesiastical milieus. . . . Marriage has a truth of its own—that is, the human knowledge, illumined by the Word of God, of the sexually different reality of the man and of the woman with their profound needs for complementarity, definitive self-giving and exclusivity—to whose discovery and deepening reason and faith harmoniously contribute.

Address to the members of the tribunal
of the Roman Rota
January 27, 2007

44. *The truth of peace* (1)

The Pastoral Constitution *Gaudium et Spes*, promulgated forty years ago at the conclusion of the Second Vatican Council, stated that mankind will not succeed in "building a truly more human world for everyone, everywhere on earth, unless all people are renewed in spirit and converted to the truth of peace" (*Gaudium et Spes*, no. 77). But what do those words, "the truth of peace," really mean? To respond adequately to this question, we must realize that peace cannot be reduced to the simple absence of armed conflict, but needs to be understood as "the fruit of an order which has been planted in human society by its divine Founder," an order "which must be brought about by humanity in its thirst for ever more perfect justice" (*Gaudium et Spes*, no. 7). As the result of an order planned and willed by the love of God, peace has an intrinsic and invincible truth of its own, and corresponds "to an irrepressible yearning and hope dwelling within us" (John Paul II, Message for the 2004 World Day of Peace, no. 9).

Message for the World Day of Peace
January 1, 2006

45. *The truth of peace* (2)

Peace! This great, heartfelt aspiration of every man and every woman is built day after day by the contribution of all and by treasuring the wonderful heritage passed down to us by the Second Vatican Council with the Pastoral Constitution *Gaudium et Spes*, which says, among other things, that humanity will not succeed in "the establishment of a truly human world for all men over the entire earth, unless everyone devotes himself to the cause of true peace with renewed vigor" (no. 77). The time in history when the Constitution *Gaudium et Spes* was promulgated, December 7, 1965, was not very different from our time. Then, as unfortunately also in our day and age, tensions of various kinds were looming on the world horizon. In the face of the lasting situations of injustice and violence that continue to oppress various parts of the earth, in the face of those that are emerging as new and more insidious threats to peace—terrorism, nihilism and fanatical fundamentalism—it is becoming more necessary than ever to work together for peace!

Homily on the Solemnity of Mary, Mother of God
January 1, 2006

46. *New approaches*

In the last part of this conciliar document in which the theme of peace among peoples is also addressed is found a basic expression on which it is good to reflect: "Peace will never be achieved once and for all, but must be built up continually" (no. 78). How true this observation is! Unfortunately, wars and violence never cease and the search for peace is always demanding. In years marked by the danger of possible global conflicts, the Second Vatican Council forcefully denounced the arms race in this text. "The arms race, which quite a few countries have entered, is no infallible way of maintaining real peace," and it immediately adds: "The arms race is one of the greatest curses on the human race and the harm it inflicts on the poor is more than can be endured" (*Gaudium et Spes*, no. 81). The Council Fathers followed this troubled observation by expressing a hope: "New approaches, based on reformed attitudes, will have to be chosen in order to remove this stumbling block, to free the earth from its pressing anxieties, and give back to the world a genuine peace" (*ibid.*). "New approaches," therefore, "based on reformed attitudes" on the renewal of minds and consciences. Today as then, authentic conversion of hearts represents the right path, the only one that can lead each one of us and all humanity to the hoped-for peace. It is the path indicated by Jesus.

> *Address to a group of young Italians, civil service*
> *volunteers, and their leaders*
> *March 28, 2009*

47. *Alpha and omega*

"Christ: Alpha and Omega" is the title of the closing paragraph of Part I of the Pastoral Constitution *Gaudium et Spes* of the Second Vatican Council, promulgated forty years ago. In that beautiful passage which borrows some words from the Servant of God Pope Paul VI, we read: "The Lord is the goal of human history, the focal point of the desires of history and civilization, the center of mankind, the joy of all hearts and the fulfillment of all aspirations. It is he whom the Father raised from the dead, exalted and placed at his right hand, constituting him judge of the living and the dead. Animated and drawn together in his Spirit we press onwards on our journey towards the consummation of history which fully corresponds to the plan of his love: "to unite all things in him, things in Heaven and things on earth" (*Gaudium et Spes*, no. 45). In light of the centrality of Christ, *Gaudium et Spes* interprets the condition of contemporary men and women, their vocation and their dignity, and also the milieus in which they live: the family, culture, the economy, politics, the international community. This is the Church's mission, yesterday, today and for ever: to proclaim and witness to Christ so that the human being, every human being, may totally fulfill his or her vocation.

Angelus
November 20, 2005

III. THE DECLARATIONS

a) *Gravissimum Educationis*[6]

48. *The way of salvation*

The Church has always been dedicated to the education of young people, recognized by the Council as something of "paramount importance" for both the life of men and women and for social progress (cf. *Gravissimum Educationis*, Preface). Today too, in an era of global communication, the Ecclesial Community perceives the importance of an educational system that recognizes the primacy of man as a person, open to truth and to good. Parents are the primary and principal educators and are assisted by civil society in accordance with the principle of subsidiarity (cf. *ibid.*, no. 3). The Church, to whom Christ entrusted the duty to proclaim the "way of salvation" (cf. *ibid.*), feels she has a special educational responsibility. In different ways, she seeks to fulfill this mission: in families, in the parish, through associations, movements and groups of formation

---

6 *Declaration on Christian Education* (October 28, 1965)

and of evangelical commitment and, in a specific way, in schools, institutes of advanced studies and in universities (cf. *ibid.*, nos. 5-12).

Angelus
October 30, 2005

b) *Nostra Aetate*[7]

49. *Interreligious dialogue*

The Declaration *Nostra Aetate* is very relevant because it regards the attitude of the Ecclesial Community in relation to non-Christian religions. Starting with the principle that "all men and women form but one community" and that the Church has the duty "to foster unity and charity" among individuals (no. 1), the Council "rejects nothing of what is true and holy" in other religions and to everyone proclaims Christ, "the way, the truth and the life," in whom men and women find the "fullness of their religious life" (no. 2). With the Declaration *Nostra Aetate* the Fathers of the Second Vatican Council proposed some fundamental truths: they clearly mentioned the special bond that joins Christians to Jews (no. 4); they confirmed their high regard for the Muslims (no. 3) and the followers of other religions (no. 2); and they confirmed the spirit of universal fraternity that rejects any form of discrimination or religious persecution (no. 5).

Angelus
October 30, 2005

---

7   *Declaration on the Relationship of the Church to Non-Christian Religions* (October 28, 1965).

50. *Brothers and sisters in God*

As the Second Vatican Council taught in the Declaration *Nostra Aetate* on the Relation of the Church to Non-Christian Religions: "We cannot truly pray to God the Father of all if we treat any people in other than brotherly fashion, for all men are created in God's image" (no. 5). Despite the differences that mark the various religious itineraries, recognition of God's existence, which human beings can only arrive at by starting from the experience of creation (cf. Rom 1:20), must dispose believers to view other human beings as brothers and sisters. It is not legitimate, therefore, for anyone to espouse religious difference as a presupposition or pretext for an aggressive attitude towards other human beings.

Message on the 20th anniversary of the Interreligious Meeting of Prayer for Peace
September 2, 2006

51. *Path*

The Second Vatican Council affirms that "all peoples are one community and have one origin, because God caused the whole human race to dwell on the face of the earth (cf. Acts 17:26); they also have one final end, God" (*Message for the World Day of Peace*, 2008, no. 1). "His providence, His manifestations of goodness, His saving design extend to all men" (Declaration *Nostra Aetate*, no. 1). Thus, "we do not live alongside one another purely by chance; all of us are progressing along a common path as men and women, and thus as brothers and sisters" (*Message for the World Day of Peace*, 2008, no. 6).

> *Message for the 97th World Day of*
> *Migrants and Refugees*
> *September 27, 2010*

52. Task

Confronted by the risk of persistent religious and cultural relativism, [the *Doctrinal Note on Some Aspects of Evangelization*] reaffirms that in the age of interreligious and intercultural dialogue the Church does not dispense with the need for evangelization and missionary activity for peoples, nor does she cease to ask men and women to accept the salvation offered to them all. Recognition of elements of truth and good in the world's religions and the seriousness of their religious endeavors, together with dialogue and a spirit of collaboration with them for the defense and promotion of the person's dignity and the universal moral values, cannot be understood as a limitation of the Church's missionary task, which involves her in ceaselessly proclaiming Christ as the Way, the Truth and the Life (cf. Jn 14:6).

> *Address to participants in the plenary session of the*
> *Congregation for the Doctrine of the Faith*
> *January 31, 2008*

c) *Dignitatis Humanae*[8]

53. The search for truth

The Council Fathers approved, precisely 40 years ago, a Declaration on the question of religious liberty, that is, the right of persons and of communities to seek the truth and to profess their faith freely. The first words that give this document its title are "*dignitatis humanae*": religious liberty derives from the special dignity of the human person, who is the only one of all the creatures on this earth who can establish a free and conscious relationship with his or her Creator. "It is in accordance with their dignity that all men, because they are persons, that is, beings endowed with reason and free will . . . , are both impelled by their nature and bound by a moral obligation to seek the truth, especially religious truth" (*Dignitatis Humanae*, no. 2). Thus, the Second Vatican Council reaffirms the traditional Catholic doctrine which holds that men and women, as spiritual creatures, can know the truth and therefore have the duty and the right to seek it (cf. *ibid.*, no. 3). Having laid this foundation, the Council places a broad emphasis on religious liberty, which must be guaranteed both to individuals and to communities with respect for the legitimate demands of the public order. And after forty years, this conciliar teaching is still most timely. Religious liberty is indeed very far from being effectively guaranteed everywhere: in certain cases it is denied for

---

8 *Declaration on Religious Freedom* (December 7, 1965).

religious or ideological reasons; at other times, although it may be recognizable on paper, it is hindered in effect by political power or, more cunningly, by the cultural predomination of agnosticism and relativism.

Angelus
December 4, 2005

IV. THE DECREES

a) *Inter Mirifica*[9]

54. *Media*

Knowledge of the value and great usefulness of the media for disseminating the Gospel and forming consciences has grown since the Second Vatican Council.

Speech
October 1, 2005

55. *Networking*

In the wake of the fortieth-anniversary of the closing of the Second Vatican Ecumenical Council, I am happy to recall its Decree on the Means of Social Communication, *Inter Mirifica*, which in particular recognized the power of the media to influence the whole of human society [and] the need to harness that power for the benefit of all mankind.

Message for the 40th World Communications Day
January 24, 2006

---

9 *Decree on the Instruments of Social Communication* (December 4, 1963).

56. *New media*

The human being . . . does not only "use" but, in a certain sense, "dwells" in language. Today, in particular, what the Second Vatican Council described as "marvelous technical inventions" (*Inter Mirifica*, no. 1) are transforming the cultural environment and this requires specific attention to the languages that are developing in it. The power of the new technologies "extends to defining not only what people will think but even what they will think about" (*Aetatis Novae*, no. 4).

> *Address to participants in the plenary assembly of the*
> *Pontifical Council for Social Communications*
> *February 28, 2011*

b) *Unitatis Redintegratio*[10]

57. *Spiritual ecumenism*

The Second Vatican Council paid great attention to the topic of Christian unity, especially in the Decree on Ecumenism (*Unitatis Redintegratio*), in which, among other things, the role and importance of prayer for unity is forcefully emphasized. Prayer, the Council observed, is at the very heart of the entire ecumenical process. "This change of heart and holiness of life, along with public and private prayer for the unity of Christians, should be regarded as the soul of the whole ecumenical movement" (*Unitatis Redintegratio*, no. 8). Thanks precisely to this spiritual ecumenism—holiness of life, conversion of heart, private and public prayer—the common search for unity has in recent decades recorded considerable development. This has been diversified in multiple initiatives: from mutual knowledge to brotherly contact between the members of different Churches and Ecclesial Communities, from ever more friendly conversations to collaboration in various fields, from theological dialogue to the search for concrete forms of communion and collaboration.

General audience
January 23, 2008

---

10 *Decree on Ecumenism* (November 21, 1964)

58. *Common prayer* (1)

Prayer for unity is part of the central nucleus which the Second Vatican Council calls "the soul of the whole ecumenical movement" (*Unitatis Redintegratio*, no. 8), a nucleus that includes public and private prayers, conversion of heart and holiness of life. This vision takes us back to the heart of the ecumenical problem, which is obedience to the Gospel in order to do God's will with his necessary and effective help. The Council explicitly pointed this out to the faithful, declaring: "The closer their union with the Father, the Word, and the Spirit, the more deeply and easily will they be able to grow in mutual brotherly love" (*ibid.*, no. 7). The elements that, despite the persistent division, still unite Christians, make it possible to raise a common prayer to God. This communion in Christ sustains the entire ecumenical movement and indicates the very purpose of the search for unity of all Christians in God's Church. It is what distinguishes the ecumenical movement from any other initiative of dialogue and relations with other religions and ideologies.

General audience
January 18, 2006

59. *Common prayer* (2)

The Council places the emphasis on prayer in common, prayer raised jointly to the one Heavenly Father by Catholics and by other Christians. The Decree on Ecumenism says in this regard: "Such prayers in common are certainly a very effective means of petitioning for the grace of unity" (*Unitatis Redintegratio*, no. 8). And this is because, in praying together, Christian communities place themselves before the Lord and, becoming aware of the contradictions to which division has given rise, manifest their desire to obey the Lord's will with trusting recourse to his almighty assistance. The Decree then adds that such prayers "are a genuine expression of the ties which still bind Catholics to their separated (*seiuncti*) brethren" (*ibid.*). Prayer in common is not, therefore, a voluntaristic or purely sociological act, but rather an expression of faith that unites all Christ's disciples.

General audience
January 23, 2008

60. *Interior conversion*

Among other things, in [the Decree *Unitatis Redintegratio*] one reads: "There can be no ecumenism worthy of the name without interior conversion. For it is from newness of attitudes of mind (cf. Eph 4:23), from self-denial and unstinted love, that desires of unity take their rise and develop in a mature way" (no. 7). The attitude of interior conversion in Christ, of spiritual renewal, of growth in charity toward other Christians has given way to a new situation in ecumenical relations. The fruits of theological dialogue, with their convergence and with the most precise identification of the divergences that still remain, urge the courageous pursuance of two directions: in the acceptance of what has been positively achieved and in a renewed commitment toward the future.

Homily for the conclusion of the Week of Prayer for Christian Unity
January 25, 2009

61. *Full unity*

The horizon of full unity remains open before us. It is an arduous duty, but stirring for Christians who want to live in harmony with the Lord's prayer: "that they may be one, that the world may believe" (Jn 17:21). The Second Vatican Council has given us the prospect of "this holy objective—the reconciliation of all Christians in the unity of the one and only Church of Christ—[which] transcends human powers and gifts" (*Unitatis Redintegratio*, no. 24). Trusting in the prayer of the Lord Jesus Christ, and encouraged by the significant steps accomplished by the ecumenical movement, let us invoke the Holy Spirit with faith so that he continues to illuminate and guide our way. May the Apostle Paul, who fatigued and suffered so much for the unity of the Mystical Body of Christ, urge us and assist us from heaven.

Homily for the conclusion of the Week of Prayer for Christian Unity
January 25, 2009

c) *Orientalium Ecclesiarum*[11]

62. *Ecumenical horizon*

For my part, I feel it is my main duty to encourage the syn-odality so dear to Eastern ecclesiology and acknowledged with appreciation by the Second Vatican Ecumenical Coun-cil. I fully share in the esteem that the Council showed your Churches in the Decree *Orientalium Ecclesiarum* which my venerable Predecessor John Paul II reaffirmed in partic-ular in his Apostolic Exhortation *Orientale Lumen*. I also share in the hope that the Eastern Catholic Churches will "flourish" in order "to fulfill with new apostolic strength the task entrusted to them," so as to foster "the unity of all Christians, in particular of Eastern Christians, accord-ing to the principles laid down in the decree of this holy Council, 'On Ecumenism'" (*Orientalium Ecclesiarum*, nos. 1, 24). The ecumenical horizon is often connected with the interreligious outlook. In these two areas the whole Church needs the experience of coexistence, which your Churches have developed since the first Christian millennium.

> *Ecumenical meeting with Eastern Catholic patriarchs*
> *and major archbishops*
> *September 19, 2009*

---

11 *Decree on Eastern Catholic Churches* (November 21, 1964).

63. *Authentic communion*

The Second Vatican Council committed the Catholic Church "irrevocably to following the path of the ecumenical venture, thus heeding the Spirit of the Lord who teaches us to interpret carefully the 'signs of the times'" (*Ut Unum Sint*, no. 3). This is the path that the Catholic Church has wholeheartedly embraced since that time. The Churches of East and West . . . share a real, if still imperfect, communion.

Address to an ecumenical delegation from Finland
January 18, 2010

d) *Optatam Totius*[12]

64. Witness

The Second Vatican Council, in speaking of the witness that awakens vocations, emphasizes the example of charity and of fraternal cooperation which priests must offer (cf. Decree *Optatam Totius*, no. 2).

Message for the 47th World Day of Prayer for Vocations
April 25, 2010

---

12 *Decree on Priestly Formation* (October 28, 1965).

e) *Perfectae Caritatis*[13]

65. Discipleship

[In remembering] the promulgation of the conciliar Decree *Perfectae Caritatis* on the renewal of religious life . . . I hope that the fundamental guidelines offered by the Council Fathers at that time for the progress of the consecrated life will also be a source of inspiration today for all who dedicate their lives to the service of the Kingdom of God. I am referring primarily to what the Decree *Perfectae Caritatis* describes as "*vitae religiosae ultima norma*," "the final norm of the religious life," that is, the "*sequela Christi*." A genuine recovery of religious life is impossible without seeking to live in complete conformity with the Gospel, without putting anything before the one Love, but finding in Christ and in his words the essence that is deeper than any Founder's or Foundress' charism.

Letter for the plenary of the Congregation for Institutes of Consecrated Life and Societies of Apostolic Life
September 27, 2005

---

13 *Decree on the Appropriate Renewal of the Religious Life* (October 28, 1965).

f) *Christus Dominus*[14]

66. *Union*

In fact, "Bishops, as legitimate successors of the Apostles and members of the Episcopal College, should appreciate that they are closely united to each other and should be solicitous for all the Churches" (*Christus Dominus*, no. 6). Yet experience tells us that this unity is never achieved once and for all and that it must be ceaselessly built up and perfected, without surrendering to the objective and subjective difficulties but rather with the determination to reveal the Catholic Church's one and only true face.

> *Address to the bishops of the*
> *Episcopal Conference of Peru*
> *May 18, 2009*

67. *Solicitude*

This spirit of communion has a privileged application in the Bishop's relationship with his priests. I am well acquainted with your desire to pay greater attention to your priests, and, in line with the Second Vatican Council, I encourage you to be solicitous, showing fatherly and brotherly love, "for the welfare spiritual, intellectual, and material of your priests, so that they may live holy and pious lives, and exercise a faithful and fruitful ministry" (*Christus Dominus*,

---

14 *Decree on the Bishops' Pastoral Office in the Church* (October 28, 1965).

no. 16). Likewise, I urge you to show charity and caution, when you have to correct teachings, attitudes or forms of behavior that do not befit the priestly condition of your closest collaborators and, moreover, could damage and confuse the faith and the Christian life of the faithful.

Address to the bishops of the
Episcopal Conference of Argentina
March 14, 2009

g) *Apostolicam Actuositatem*[15]

68. *Lay faithful*

On November 18, 1965, the Fathers approved a specific Decree on the Apostolate of Lay People, *Apostolicam Actuositatem*. It stressed first of all that "the fruitfulness of the apostolate of lay people depends on their living union with Christ" (no. 4), that is, on a vigorous spirituality nourished by active participation in the Liturgy and expressed in the style of the Gospel Beatitudes. For lay people, moreover, professional competence, a sense of family, a civic sense and the social virtues are of great importance. Although it is true that they are called individually to bear their personal witness, particularly precious wherever the freedom of the Church encounters obstacles, the Council nonetheless insisted on the importance of the organized apostolate, essential if an effect is to be made on the general mindset, social conditions and institutions (cf. *ibid.*, no. 18).

Angelus
November 13, 2005

69. *Apostolate*

The Second Vatican Council's vision is that wherever the lay faithful live out their baptismal vocation—in the family, at home, at work—they are actively participating in the Church's mission to sanctify the world. A renewed focus

---

15 *Decree on the Apostolate of the Laity* (November 18, 1965).

on *lay apostolate* will help to clarify the roles of clergy and laity and so give a strong impetus to the task of evangelizing society.

> *Address to the bishops of the*
> *Episcopal Conference of Scotland*
> *February 5, 2010*

70. *Lay associations*

The Ecclesial Movements and New Communities are one of the most important innovations inspired by the Holy Spirit in the Church for the implementation of the Second Vatican Council. They spread in the wake of the Council sessions especially in the years that immediately followed it, in a period full of exciting promises but also marked by difficult trials. . . . Indeed, even then [the new lay groups] were already bearing witness to the joy, reasonableness and beauty of being Christian, showing that they were grateful for belonging to the mystery of communion which is the Church. We have witnessed the reawakening of a vigorous missionary impetus, motivated by the desire to communicate to all the precious experience of the encounter with Christ, felt and lived as the only adequate response to the human heart's profound thirst for truth and happiness.

> *Address to bishops and representatives of ecclesial*
> *movements and new communities*
> *May 17, 2008*

h) *Ad Gentes*[16]

71. *Ways*

Many [are the] ways inspired by the Holy Spirit with the Second Vatican Council for the new evangelization.

> *Address to members of the Neocatechumenal Way*
> *of the Diocese of Rome*
> *January 10, 2009*

72. *Mission*

The Church is by nature missionary; her urgent duty is to evangelize. The Second Vatican Council dedicated to missionary activity the Decree entitled, precisely, "*Ad Gentes*." It recalls that "the Apostles . . . following the footsteps of Christ, 'preached the word of truth and begot churches' (St. Augustine, *Enarr. in Ps.* 44, 23: *PL* 36, 508; *CChr.* 30, 510)," and that it "is the duty of their successors to carry on this work so that "'the word of God may run and be glorified' (2 Thes 3:1) and the Kingdom of God proclaimed and renewed throughout the whole world" (*Ad Gentes*, no. 1).

> *Homily at Mass at the Roman basilica of*
> *St. Paul Outside the Walls*
> *April 25, 2005*

---

16 *Decree on the Church's Missionary Activity* (December 7, 1965).

i) *Presbyterorum Ordinis*[17]

73. *Ecclesial communion*

Harvesting the pastoral experience of past centuries, the Second Vatican Council highlighted the importance of educating future priests to an authentic ecclesial communion. In this regard, we read in *Presbyterorum Ordinis*: "Exercising the office of Christ, the shepherd and head, according to their share of his authority, the priests, in the name of the Bishop, gather the family of God together as a brotherhood enlivened by one spirit. Through Christ they lead them in the Holy Spirit to God the Father" (no. 6). . . . It is indispensable that, within the Christian people, every ministry and charism be directed to full communion; and it is the duty of the Bishop and priests to promote this communion in harmony with every other Church vocation and service.

Message for the 44th World Day of Prayer for Vocations
April 29, 2007

74. *Co-responsibility*

I believe that this is one of the important and positive results of the Council: the co-responsibility of the entire parish, for the parish priest is no longer the only one to animate everything. Since we all form a parish together, we must all collaborate and help so that the parish priest is not left on his own, mainly as a coordinator, but truly discovers

---

17 *Decree on the Ministry and Life of Priests* (December 7, 1965).

that he is a pastor who is backed up in these common tasks in which, together, the parish lives and is fulfilled. Thus, I would say that, on the one hand, this coordination and vital responsibility for the whole parish, and on the other, the sacramental life and preaching as a center of parish life, could also today, in circumstances which are of course more difficult, make it possible to be a parish priest who may not know each person by name, as the Lord says of the Good Shepherd, but one who really knows his sheep and is really their pastor who calls and guides them.

Address at the meeting with clergy of the Dioceses of Belluno-Feltre and Treviso July 24, 2007

75. *Priestly continuity*

Just as the hermeneutics of continuity are proving ever more urgent for a satisfactory understanding of the Second Vatican Council's texts, likewise a hermeneutic we might describe as "of priestly continuity" appears necessary. This has come down to our day, starting from Jesus of Nazareth, Lord and Christ, and passing through the 2,000 years of the history of greatness and holiness, of culture and devotion which the Priesthood has written in the world.

Address to participants in the conference organized by the Congregation for the Clergy March 12, 2010

76. Reception

It is important to encourage in priests, especially in the young generations, a correct reception of the texts of the Second Ecumenical Vatican Council, interpreted in the light of the Church's entire fund of doctrine.

Address to participants in the plenary assembly of the Congregation for the Clergy March 16, 2009

V. THE CONCILIAR MESSAGES

77. *"To Rulers" and "To Men of Thought and Science"*

Dear brothers and sisters, let us return to that special moment of grace, the conclusion of the Second Vatican Council on December 8, 1965, when the Council Fathers addressed certain "Messages" to all humanity. The first was addressed "To Rulers" and the second, "To Men of Thought and Science." These are two categories of people who, in a certain way, we can see portrayed in the evangelical figures of the Magi. I would then like to add a third category, to which the Council did not address a message but which was very present in its attention in the conciliar Decree *Nostra Aetate.* I am referring to the spiritual leaders of the great non-Christian religions. . . . Today, I would like to make my own those Messages of the Council which have lost nothing of their timeliness. For instance, one reads in the Message addressed to Rulers: "Your task is to be in the world the promoters of order and peace among men. But never forget this: It is God, the living and true God, who is the Father of men. And it is Christ, his eternal Son, who came to make this known to us and to teach us that we are all brothers. He it is who is the great artisan of order and peace on earth, for he it is who guides human history and who alone can incline hearts to renounce those evil passions which beget war and misfortune." How can we fail to recognize in these words of the Council Fathers the luminous trail of a journey which alone can transform the history of the nations and the world? And further, in the "Message to Men of Thought and Science" we read: "Continue your search without tiring and without ever despairing of the truth," and this, in fact, is the great danger: losing interest in the truth and seeking only action, efficiency and pragmatism! "Recall the words of one of your great friends, St. Augustine: 'Let us seek with the desire to find, and find with the desire to seek still more.' Happy are those who, while possessing the truth, search more earnestly for it in order to renew it, deepen it and transmit it to others. Happy also are those who, not having found it, are working toward it with a sincere heart. May they seek the light of tomorrow with the light of today until they reach the fullness of light." This was said in these two Council Messages. Today, it is more necessary than ever to flank the leaders of nations and researchers and scientists with the leaders of the great non-Christian religious traditions, inviting them to face one another with the light of Christ, who came not to abolish but to bring to fulfillment what God's hand has written in the religious history of civilization, especially in the "great souls" who helped to build up humanity with their wisdom and example of virtue. Christ is light, and light cannot darken but can only illuminate, brighten, reveal.

Homily on the Solemnity of the Epiphany
January 6, 2007

78. *"To the Poor, the Sick, and the Suffering"*

The Second Ecumenical Vatican Council had already recalled the Church's important task of caring for human suffering. In the Dogmatic Constitution *Lumen Gentium* we read that "Christ was sent by the Father 'to bring good news to the poor . . . to heal the contrite of heart' (Lk 4:18), 'to seek and to save what was lost' (Lk 19:10). . . . Similarly, the Church encompasses with her love all those who are afflicted by human misery and she recognizes in those who are poor and who suffer, the image of her poor and suffering Founder. She does all in her power to relieve their need and in them she strives to serve Christ" (no. 8). . . . I am anxious to add that at this moment in history and culture we are feeling even more acutely the need for an attentive and far-reaching ecclesial presence beside the sick, as well as a presence in society that can effectively pass on the Gospel values that safeguard human life in all its phases, from its conception to its natural end. I would like here to take up the *Message to the Poor, the Sick, and the Suffering* which the Council Fathers addressed to the world at the end of the Second Ecumenical Vatican Council: "All of you who feel heavily the weight of the Cross," they said, "you who weep . . . you the unknown victims of suffering, take courage. You are the preferred children of the Kingdom of God, the Kingdom of hope, happiness, and life. You are the brothers of the suffering Christ, and with him, if you wish, you are saving the world" (*The Documents of Vatican II*, Walter M. Abbott, SJ).

Message for the 18th World Day of the Sick
November 22, 2009

INDEX

*(Numbering refers to the sequential
positioning of each thought.)*

Culture: 41, 47, 77

Dei Verbum: 26-34

Dignitatis Humanae: 53

Ecclesial movements: 22, 70

Economy: 47

Ecumenism: 57-63

    and interior conversion, 60

    prayer for, 58-59

    spiritual, 57

Education: 48

Eucharist

    table of the Word and the Body and Blood of Christ, 29

Evangelization: 52, 71-72

Faith tradition: 9

Family: 47

Gaudium et Spes: 35-47

God

    brotherhood in, 50

    fear of, 35

    transcendence of, 37

    ultimate end, 51

Gravissimum Educationis: 48

Inter Mirifica: 54-56

Interreligious dialogue: 49-52, 62, 77

Jesus Christ

    centrality of, 2, 47

    discipleship, 39

    in the liturgy, 10

Laity: 21, 68-69

Lectio divina: 31